Hickory
Dickory Dock

Hickory

Dickory Dock

Adapted and Illustrated by
Marilyn Janovitz

Hyperion Books for Children

For Ellen and baby Zak

First Edition
10 9 8 7 6 5 4 3 2 1

Library of Congress Cataloging-in-Publication Data
Janovitz, Marilyn.
Hickory dickory dock / adapted and illustrated by Marilyn Janovitz.
p. cm.
Summary: In this illustrated version of the old nursery rhyme,
mice scamper around a cat's shop and take his lunch
while he is napping.
ISBN 1-56282-083-4 (trade)—ISBN 1-56282-084-2 (library)
1. Nursery rhymes. 2. Children's poetry. [1. Nursery rhymes.] I. Title.
PZ8.3.J263Hi 1991 398.8—dc20 91-71378 CIP AC

The artwork for each picture consists of watercolor and colored pencil,
and is prepared on Arches watercolor paper.

The text is set in 24pt. ITC Clearface.

WATCH CAT'S
CLOCK SHOP

Hickory!

Dickory!   Dock!

The mouse ran

up the clock.

The clock

struck one,

the mouse

ran down,

Hickory!

Dickory! Dock!

Hick-o-ry, dick-o-ry dock! The

mouse ran up the clock. The

clock struck one, the mouse ran down,

Hick-o-ry, dick-o-ry dock!